Methuen Drama Modern Classics

Methuen Drama's *Modern Classics* series showcases landmark plays from around the world. Drawing on the *Modern Plays* series, which launched in 1959, *Modern Classics* celebrates plays from the contemporary repertoire by world-leading dramatists and presents their work in a definitive edition, alongside new introductions by leading scholars and industry professionals. With writers such as Pulitzer Prize-winners Jackie Sibblies Drury, Ayad Akhtar and David Mamet through to Lucy Prebble, Katori Hall and Caryl Churchill, *Modern Classics* are ideal for students and anyone wanting to deepen their knowledge of the plays that form part of the modern dramatic canon.

Desdemona

'This is a remarkable, challenging and bravely original work.'
The Guardian

Ripped from the world by her husband's paranoia, Desdemona turns in death towards the memory of Barbary, the North African maid who raised her: together, they explore the contours of death, race, war, love and motherhood, in a moving elegy.

Audacious with ambition, *Desdemona* is Toni Morrison's intimate reimagining of the fourth act of Shakespeare's *Othello*, mixing monologue with Rokia Traoré's lyrical songs to re-examine the Bard's presentation of race and female suffering.

Part-play, part-concert, part-quest into the afterlife, *Desdemona* is published in Methuen Drama's Modern Classics series, featuring a new introduction by Joyce Green MacDonald.

T0027099

Toni Morrison was a Nobel Prize- and Pulitzer Prize-winning novelist, editor and professor. Her novels are known for their epic themes, exquisite language and richly detailed African American characters who are central to their narratives. Among her best-known novels are *The Bluest Eye*, *Sula*, *Song of Solomon*, *Beloved*, *Jazz*, *Love* and *A Mercy*. Morrison earned a plethora of book-world accolades and honorary degrees, also receiving the Presidential Medal of Freedom in 2012.

Desdemona

Toni Morrison
Lyrics by Rokia Traoré

With an introduction by Joyce Green MacDonald

methuen | drama
LONDON · NEW YORK · OXFORD · NEW DELHI · SYDNEY

METHUEN DRAMA
Bloomsbury Publishing Plc
50 Bedford Square, London, WC1B 3DP, UK
1385 Broadway, New York, NY 10018, USA
29 Earlsfort Terrace, Dublin 2, Ireland

BLOOMSBURY, METHUEN DRAMA and the Methuen Drama logo
are trademarks of Bloomsbury Publishing Plc

First published in Great Britain by Methuen Drama in 2012
This Modern Classics edition published in 2024

Cover design: Ben Anslow

A catalogue record for this book is available from the British Library.

A catalog record for this book is available from the Library of Congress.

ISBN: PB: 978-1-3504-2898-0
ePDF: 978-1-3504-2900-0
eBook: 978-1-3504-2899-7

Series: Modern Classics

Typeset by Newgen KnowledgeWorks Pvt. Ltd., Chennai, India
Printed and bound in Great Britain

To find out more about our authors and books visit www.bloomsbury.com
and sign up for our newsletters.

Contents

Introduction

Since its premiere in 1604, *Othello* has seized its audiences and not let go. One measure of the power the play continues to hold over us is the vast number of adaptations and revisions it has inspired. In the nineteenth century, minstrel show versions sought to undermine its tragic grandeur by transforming its poetry and its portrait of an inevitably doomed romance between a privileged white Venetian woman and an African general into objects of ridicule. Twentieth-century versions have remade the play in ways that blast its enshrinement of patriarchal value (e.g. Paula Vogel's 1993 *Desdemona, A Play About a Handkerchief*), or try their hardest to avoid its seeming foreordained stereotype of Black male violence; Basil Dearden's 1963 film *All Night Long* has its Othello and Desdemona figures resolve their crisis of jealousy and go on together. But rather than try to undo the treatments of race and gender and social status that can make *Othello* such an unbearably fraught experience in the theatre, Toni Morrison's *Desdemona* (2011) turns these fractures into the centre of her bold reimagining of Shakespeare's text. By inviting us into the afterlife of Shakespeare's characters and inventing opportunities for them to explain themselves and to speak to each other – even inventing characters when she must – she invites us to break *Othello*'s hold.

In the classroom, I have found that new readers of Shakespeare's play are often frustrated by the fact that Iago can get away with so much. Taking him at face value as 'honest' Iago, the other characters don't realize how vicious he really is until it's too late. Coming to her work on *Othello*, Morrison experienced the same frustration: Iago is 'everywhere, he's talking constantly, nobody's telling him the truth, he's manipulating everybody, he's gobbling up the play and nobody can just live'.[1] The first and greatest liberty *Desdemona* takes with Shakespeare is to get rid of the character of Iago. Without his distracting and deceptive presence, the play's survivors can finally and simply speak and listen to each other. This is not to say that without him, *Desdemona* avoids tragedy: it does not. Its Othello and Desdemona still die. What does become possible, however, is the kind of understanding and insight that the breakneck pace of Shakespeare's play cannot let its characters achieve.

Speaking from an eternal world beyond the grave, beyond the unforgiving social structures of Venice or Cyprus, Morrison's characters are freed to fill in some of the background about themselves and their relationships to each other that remain hidden or unvoiced in Shakespeare. Desdemona tells us about the constrained, dutiful upbringing that conflicted with the 'unseemliness' of her own childhood imagination (p. 7). We know from Shakespeare's play that she is capable of going against her father's wishes, but from Morrison we learn that this natural rebelliousness grew in opposition to the childhood strictures imposed on her by her mother, whose job it was to train her to become a proper Venetian lady. The training could be cruel. When ten-year-old Desdemona lost her slippers and soaked the hem of her gown trying to imitate the swans that swam in her family's pond, her mother's response was to make her go barefoot for ten days, one day for each year of her life. Desdemona compares the punishment to 'a dark, heavy curtain' (p. 7), but also tells us that it only made her cleave to her natural rebelliousness all the more. The young woman who contracts the runaway marriage to Othello is her mother's child perhaps more than her father's, regardless of what Shakespeare tells us, formed in natural reaction to the imposed rules of aristocratic ladyhood that she was forced to learn at her mother's knee.

Morrison widens Desdemona's conflicted memory of her mother into a greater meditation on motherhood and loss when she brings her invented characters Madam Brabantio and Soun, Othello's mother, onstage together. In Shakespeare, Othello is deeply shaped by the absent African women who moulded his character and taught him that romantic love can be tenuous and hurtful: the unnamed mother who gave him the strawberry-embroidered handkerchief, the Egyptian 'charmer' who'd given it to her, the prophetess who crafted it. The kinds of symbolic authority and influence Shakespeare gives Black female characters – or, more often, the idea of Black femininity – contrasts sharply with their common physical absence from his stage. They don't have to be in front of us to matter to the ways in which his characters imagine aspiration, impossibility, unattainable beauty, immutable sexual degradation. But when Morrison brings Othello's mother onstage with Desdemona's, she not only voices and visualizes a part of this terrible story that Shakespeare does not, but also uses Soun's responses to their shared loss as a map to a range of social and emotional formations that shaped her son as much as the force of Venetian custom shaped Desdemona. Madam Brabantio asks Soun to kneel with her at their children's graves, but Soun refuses. 'I come from a land wildly different from yours,' she tells Desdemona's mother. 'There we obey nature and look to it for the language of the gods' (p. 17). Part of this divine reception is the assurance that people can survive grief and loss. Nothing, Soun implies, is ever as final as the end of *Othello*, where the sight of the 'tragic loading' of Othello and Desdemona's wedding bed is so painful and unjust that it cannot be borne. 'Let it be hid', Lodovico orders there. Instead, Soun says that her people build altars in the face of loss, summoning 'the spirits who are waiting to console us' (p. 17). In the eternal afterlife of *Desdemona*, even cruel death is not the end.

This modulation of the terrible tragedy of *Othello* strikes me as a central part of Morrison's response to Shakespeare. Again, her play doesn't avoid or evade tragedy; rather, *Desdemona* argues that human connection – the kind of connection that Iago's busy plotting prevents the other characters from building – is a powerful and necessary means of 'diluting the poisons life forces us to swallow' (p. 17). Tragedy will come, but we can bear it. In the contemplative afterlife where her play takes place, her characters speak the truth that will help them understand and accept what has happened and how their lives brought them here. They have, Morrison remarked, 'everything to learn' from each other and about themselves, and 'nothing to lose'.[2]

Part of what Morrison's Desdemona learns is that her experiences and perceptions are not the only ones that matter. Not only malice but our own solipsism can keep us from forging the human connection that is our only protection from suffering. She lovingly remembers her mother's maid Barbary, whose name evokes the North African territories that help detail *Othello*'s interest in the contrast between civilized Venice and its barbarian outlands. Barbary was the one who 'conspired with' her young charge to let her imagination roam. 'She tended me as though she were my birth mother: braided my hair, dressed me, comforted me when I was ill and danced with me when I recovered' (p. 8). Yet, when Desdemona delightedly encounters Barbary after their deaths, she finds out that the truth of their relationship was not what she remembers. 'Barbary' was not even her name; her real name was Sa'ran, and 'Barbary' only the label assigned her, 'the geography of the foreigner, the savage ... the name of those without whom you could not prosper' (p. 35). She was not, could not have been the warm friend that Desdemona remembers, because she had been a slave in Brabantio's household, 'the sly, vicious enemy who must be put down at any price; held down for the conquerors' pleasure' (p. 35). The privilege Desdemona still enjoyed despite her own discomfort under her parents' rule blinded her to the hidden forced labour that made her life possible.

Morrison underlines Desdemona's lack of comprehension by reclaiming the 'Willow Song' she sings in *Othello* the night her husband murders her. Or rather, Shakespeare's Desdemona tries to sing the song of romantic betrayal she had often heard Barbary sing when she was a girl, but she cannot remember all the words. The moment maps Desdemona's heartbreak over her (faulty) memory of Barbary's song; she does not fully grasp the details or substance of the original performance, yet is certain as only a pampered child could be that Barbary's experience is somehow hers to claim. In *Desdemona*, just as Sa'ran corrects Desdemona's understanding of what their relationship had been, she also rejects the possibility of identification with her experience that she believes she heard in the song. Even though Desdemona was also betrayed by the man she loved and never hurt Sa'ran (although Sa'ran apparently did suffer unnamed abuse in Brabantio's house), her experience was not, could not be the same, and is not available for Desdemona to claim as her own. In the afterlife, Sa'ran is free to declare a new identity free of pain and appropriation. Her new song declares that

> a sudden breath caresses
> The salt my eyes have shed.
> And I hear a call – clear, so clear:
> 'You will never die again.'   (39)

Desdemona's interest in the relationships between *Othello*'s women – those who appear in the play (Emilia, Bianca) and those who do not (Madam Brabantio, Soun, Sa'ran) – mark an important axis along which Morrison reframes Shakespeare. She wants to tell us what the play leaves out, finding in this information about Desdemona's nurture a vibrant guide to the emotional field in which the play might alternatively take place. As it reframes Shakespeare's Desdemona, Morrison's play also tells us more about Othello himself, remaking the Moor into a character with a personal history more desperate and terrible than the exotic backstory Shakespeare gives us. If her Desdemona had chafed under the controls of domesticity and respectable womanhood, Morrison's Othello had never known a home. He had been an enslaved child soldier, drugged and inured to violence in worlds without mercy. He and the other boys 'were potent and indifferent to blood, cries of pain, debasement – to life, even our own. Rape was perfunctory. Death our brother' (p. 26). Desdemona now believes that he always knew Iago was lying to him but that the recognition that Iago offered him – the recognition of the bond that a shared history of violence and cruelty and exile from human sympathy could forge – was too difficult to reject in a life so bereft of connection. Iago was the only one who knew and understood his past until Othello confessed to Desdemona in the afterlife. 'The wide, wild celebrity men find with each other cannot compete with the narrow comfort of a wife,' she remarks (p. 27). Their romance was always doomed by forces beyond Othello's control, forces and influences that Morrison imagines while Shakespeare does not.

Morrison's Othello tells Desdemona that he and Iago had once raped a pair of old women while a horrified child – the grandson of one of them? – watched. Together, they had taken pleasure in the 'degradation' (p. 28) they inflicted on their victims and in having made someone else that degradation's unwilling witness. Forcing the child to watch displaced his own shame and fear over what he had become onto another victim, a victim as helpless as he himself had once been. Desdemona cannot forgive him such crimes. She tells him, 'But I can love you and remain committed to you' (p. 29). In place of the rapturous romance that sweeps Shakespeare's characters into the abyss, Morrison offers a considered, deliberate choice: 'Honest love does not cringe at the first roll of thunder; nor does it flinch when faced with the lightning flash of human sin' (p. 29). In life, Desdemona believed that he was more than the tormented 'visage' (p. 29) of himself that he carried in his own mind. Now, he tells her, he prays he can be.

As it speaks across time and death, supplying detail that Shakespeare's play does not or cannot, *Desdemona* also uses theatrical methods that move beyond conventional dialogue and discovery. Malian musician Rokia Traoré was an instrumental part of the play's first performances, leading a small ensemble onstage and who sang and played accompaniment to and commentary on the play's action. Using West African instruments, framing her lyrics in light of African cultural tradition, Traoré's contributions underline *Desdemona*'s interest in detailing the world that shaped Othello as well as providing an alternate framing of the customs and assumptions that Shakespeare's play takes for granted. In a song offered as a kind of prayer for Othello as he and Desdemona fall in love, for example, Traoré's ensemble sing

> Othello, a great man
> does not give in to anger.
> Contain your rage.
> Let a river of peace
> flow through you,
> the serenity of a breeze
> from the prairies.   (14)

Later, after Desdemona has told him that she still loves him despite what he did, the lyrics express his fear that she will leave him:

> Grant me the time I need
> for wisdom
> to grow in me
> and give me the strength
> to smile at my pain.
> Don't leave me.   (31)

Desdemona works to make Shakespeare's *Othello* less opaque by imagining a fuller background for its conflicts and characters. Traoré's score is integral to this effort as it sonically and lyrically locates the play outside a world governed by the assumptions – racial, hierarchical, sexual – of Shakespeare's Venice.

More than four hundred years ago, Shakespeare's *Othello* initiated a conversation about race and sex and social status, a one-sided conversation that has frequently found it difficult to acknowledge perspectives originating from outside a white and Western and patriarchal status quo. Nevertheless, and perhaps because of the apparent finality of those conclusions, later writers have insisted on questioning and answering *Othello*. Morrison's *Desdemona* earns its place among these creative responses, I think, because of what it doesn't try to do. It's not interested in denying the grief and pity at the heart of its original. But even if Morrison's reimagined tragedy accepts that Othello and Desdemona are in some ways destined to die, it refuses to accept as inevitably true the mass of racist assumptions that have been marshalled over the long theatrical life of the play, and in its text, in order to explain their fates. (As early as 1818, Samuel Coleridge Taylor found it unbelievable that a 'beautiful Venetian girl' and a 'veritable Negro' could fall in love, and suggested that Othello wasn't really supposed to be Black.) Rather, in building new histories for her characters, new inner lives, new moments of honesty and emotional learning, Morrison readies an alternative ground for understanding them and their story. Her play's afterworld/aftertime grants them the peace and the patience to hear the origins of the racial stories that Shakespeare's original decreed must be left hidden. In so doing, she invites her audience to see Othello and Desdemona in a new light.

Joyce Green MacDonald

Notes

1   From a 2014 interview with Professor Jerry Brotton, https://www.youtube. com/watch?v=1-k-O2yLYOo.

2   Ibid.

Desdemona

Desdemona was commissioned and co-produced by Wiener Festwochen, Théâtre Nanterre-Amandiers, Cal Performances, Berkeley, California, Lincoln Center for the Performing Arts, New York, spielzeit'europa I Berliner Festspiele, and Barbican, London, Arts Council London and London 2012 Festival.

The premiere performance took place on 15 May, 2011 at the Akzent Theater in Vienna, Austria.

Desdemona (Premiere)

Toni Morrison, Text

Rokia Traoré, Music and Barbary

Peter Sellars, Director

Elizabeth Marvel, Desdemona*

Mamah Diabaté, Ngoni

Fatim Kouyaté, Vocals

Bintou Soumbounou, Vocals

Naba Aminata Traoré Touré, Vocals

Mamadyba Camara, Kora

James F. Ingalls, Lighting Design

Alexis Giraud, Sound Design

Anne Dechêne, Production Stage Manager

Janet Y. Takami, Assistant Stage Manager

Diane J. Malecki, Producer

*Tina Benko in Nanterre, Berkeley,
New York, Berlin and London

1.

DESDEMONA   My name is Desdemona. The word,
Desdemona, means misery. It means ill
fated. It means doomed. Perhaps my parents
believed or imagined or knew my fortune
at the moment of my birth. Perhaps being
born a girl gave them all they needed to
know of what my life would be like. That it
would be subject to the whims of my elders
and the control of men. Certainly that was
the standard, no, the obligation of females
in Venice when I was a girl. Men made the
rules; women followed them. A step away
was doom, indeed, and misery without relief.
My parents, keenly aware and approving of
that system, could anticipate the future of a
girl child accurately.

They were wrong. They knew the system,
but they did not know me.

I am not the meaning of a name I did not
choose.

DESDEMONA
Small, uninhabited,
envious of manhood,
weakened.
You are unworthy of the femininity
that you haven't recognized in yourself,
that you distort,
that elevates and softens
your sad bitterness.
Though it feels strong,
beautiful and worthy,
we see your confusion,
sadness and hurt.

Mona, Desdemona

I exist in between, now: between being killed
and being un-dead; between life on earth
and life beyond it; between all time, which
has no beginning and no end, and all space
which is both a seedling as well as the sun it
yearns for. All that is available to me. I join
the underwater women; stroll with them
in dark light, listen to their music in the
spangled deep. Colors down there are more
violent than any produced by the sun. I live
in the roots and heads of trees. I rise in art,
in masks, in figures, in drumbeat, in fire.
I exist in places where I can speak, at last,
words that in earth life were sealed or twisted
into the language of obedience. Yes, my
Lord. By your leave, Sir.

If you had been a man
you could hardly have achieved more,
accomplished more.
Manhood in itself is not a plus.
Womanhood never imagined itself as an obstacle.
'Girl' does not know how to be less than 'boy'.
Together, they were chosen
to give meaning to life.

Is it a question of deciding
who is strongest?
Between He
who represents strength
and She
in whom all strength is rooted,
grows,
and is given meaning
and purpose?

Mona, Desdemona

Who is greater?
He, who claims supremacy
here below,
or She,
without whom there would be
no life
here below?

Mona, Desdemona

How can you confuse
finesse with obedience,
discretion with ignorance,
tenderness with submission,
seductiveness with prostitution,
woman with weakness?

Did you imagine me as a wisp of a girl?
A coddled doll who fell in love with a
handsome warrior who rode off with her
under his arm? Is it your final summation of
me that I was a foolish naïf who surrendered
to her husband's brutality because she had
no choice? Nothing could be more false.

It is true my earth life held sorrow. Yet
none of it, not one moment was 'misery'.
Difficulty, yes. Confusion, yes. Error in
judgment, yes. Murder, yes. But it was my
life and, right or wrong, my life was shaped
by my own choices and it was mine.

2.

My mother was a lady of virtue whose
practice and observation of manners were
flawless. She taught me how to handle myself
at table, how to be courteous in speech,
when and how to drop my eyes, smile,
curtsey. As was the custom, she did not
tolerate dispute from a child, nor involve
herself in what could be called my interior
life. There were strict rules of deportment,
solutions for every problem a young
girl could have. And there was sensible
punishment designed for each impropriety.
Constraint was the theme of behavior.
Duty was its plot.

I remember once splashing barefoot in
our pond, pretending I was one of the
swans that swam there. My slippers were
tossed aside; the hem of my dress wet. My
unleashed laughter was long and loud.
The unseemliness of such behavior in a
girl of less than one decade brought my
mother's attention. Too old, she scolded,
for such carelessness. To emphasize the
point, my slippers were taken away and I
remained barefoot for ten days. It was a
small thing, embarrassing, inconvenient, but
definitely clarifying. It meant my desires, my
imagination must remain hidden. It was as
though a dark heavy curtain enclosed me.
Yet wrapping that curtain over my willfulness
served to strengthen it.

My solace in those early days lay with my
nurse, Barbary. She alone encouraged a slit
in that curtain. Barbary alone conspired with
me to let my imagination run free. She told
me stories of other lives, other countries.
Places where gods speak in thundering
silence and mimic human faces and forms.
Where nature is not a crafted, pretty thing,
but wild, sacred and instructive. Unlike the
staid, unbending women of my country, she
moved with the fluid grace I saw only in
swans and the fronds of willow trees. To hear
Barbary sing was to wonder at the mediocrity
of flutes and pipes. She was more alive than
anyone I knew and more loving. She tended
me as though she were my birth mother:
braided my hair, dressed me, comforted me
when I was ill and danced with me when I
recovered. I loved her. Her heart, so wide,
seemed to hold the entire world in awe and
to savor its every delight.

Yet that same heart, wide as it was, proved
vulnerable. When I needed her most, she
stumbled under the spell of her lover. He
forsook her and turned her ecstasy into ash.
Eyes pooled with tears, she sang her loss of
him, of love, and life.

M'BIFO
I thought that strength was in unity.
I thought that having you at my side
could keep me far from my solitude
and my fears

Now, I feel lost.
Now I know that love
can be a source of evil.
I love you.
I forgive you.

I forgot my solitude for a while.
I wanted to be with you, forever.
My outstretched hands waiting to be filled
are empty of disillusion.

My melancholy thoughts are back.
But I still love the idea of love.

Her spacious heart drained and sere, Barbary
died. I mourned her so deeply, it trembled
me. And yet, even in grief I questioned:
were we women so frail in the wake of
men who swore they cherished us? Was a
lover's betrayal more lethal than betrayal
of oneself? I did not know the answers, so
I determined to be otherwise. I determined
to search most carefully for the truth of a
lover before committing my own fidelity.
That determination was a blow to my father,
Senator Brabantio. His sole interest in me as
I grew into womanhood was making certain
I was transferred, profitably and securely,
into the hands of another man.

3.

With my father's invitations, and according
to his paternal duty, I was courted by many
men. They came into my father's house with
empty ornate boxes designed to hold coins
of dowry gold, or deeds of property. They
glanced at me and locked their glistening
eyes on my father's.

Showing their teeth in doting smiles they
slid in soft shoes on our marble floor. One
by one they came in velvet and fur-trimmed
silk, prettified hats stitched with silver thread.
Each one, whether a stuttering boy or an
aged widower, was eager for a chatelaine
weighted with riches. I was thought beautiful,
but if I were not, even if I were a giantess,
a miniature or a horse-faced shrew, suitors
cruising for a bride would have sought my
hand. Those already wealthy ranked me
with other virgins on their menu. Those in
desperate straits needed no evaluation.

My father instructed me on the virtues
of each offer and when I first refused he
thought me fastidious. With my next refusal,
he chastised me as stubborn; finally, as the
refusals continued, as an embarrassment: a
single female of a certain age, un-nunned,
sitting at his sumptuous table instead of
fasting in a convent.

I had reached the cusp of unmarriageability
– that lightless abyss into which a family can
fall – burdened by an eating mouth, tied to
a poor unseeded womb, disconnected from
the chain that the clan pays out to increase its
length and its profit.

Yet my flaw was more serious than pride.
It was revolt. I yearned for talk, for meaning,
for winds from a wider world. Seas beyond
canals, populations living other ways,
speaking languages of music and roar, beasts
and gods unimagined within these walls.
I longed for adventure out there, yes, but
inside as well. Adventure in my mind no less
than in my heart.

4.

One evening I veiled my surliness and
attended another of my father's endless
banquets.

Not yet recovered from Barbary's death, I
sat mute among the guests. Bountifully fed,
they began to dance – partnered, formal,
predictably flirtatious. Hoping to exit the
mockery, I stood and moved toward my
father to ask to be excused. Among those
huddled around his chair was this mass of
a man. Tree tall. Glittering in metal and red
wool. A commander's helmet under his arm.
As I approached, he turned to let me pass.
I saw a glint of brass in his eyes identical to
the light in Barbary's eyes. I looked away,
but not before his smile summoned my
own. I don't remember what I murmured
to my father to explain my approach. I was
introduced to the Commander; he kissed
my hand, held it and requested a dance. 'By
your leave, Senator Brabantio?' In accented
language his voice underscored the kiss.

We danced together, our bodies moving
in such harmony it was as though we had
known each other all our lives.

OTHELLO
By the grace of God
destiny smiles upon you.
The wishes of your grandparents
have been exalted and fulfilled.
Great Othello,
handsome Othello
only your anger
can make you lose
yourself.
Othello, a great man
does not give in to anger.
Contain your rage.
Let a river of peace
flow through you,
the serenity of a breeze
from the prairies.
Man should not make ugly
that which is beautiful
by the will of God.
No one should despise
what God wished to be desirable.
Do not allow the anger
to open in you
a fault that makes
your misfortune.
Othello, Othello
hold back your fury.
One does not destroy
what one loves.
One does not destroy
because one loves.

OTHELLO   Come to me Desdemona. Here on this bed
               let us make a world.

DESDEMONA   You will teach me?

OTHELLO   If you know how to laugh you will not need
               lessons. Desire is nature's purest gift.

DESDEMONA   And what is in this world we will make?

OTHELLO   Singing children watching men like me,
               warriors needing love, put down their swords
               to dance.

DESDEMONA   And women?

OTHELLO   Like you. With eyes than cannot hide
               the mind's sharp intelligence; a throat
               demanding my lips; shoulders inviting
               caresses; strawberry nipples hiding a bold
               and loving heart.

DESDEMONA   And laughter is our teacher?

OTHELLO   And our flesh is its lesson.

DESDEMONA   Then let my flesh be re-born through yours.

OTHELLO   Having captured glee, we melt and become
               one.

DESDEMONA   I adore you.

OTHELLO   I love you. Turn away old world, while my
               love and I create a new one.

5.

Two women approach each other. One is dressed in simple cloth, the other in a sumptuous gown. They both have white hair and carry a torch.

M. BRABANTIO   'Who are you?'

SOUN   'My name is Soun, and you?'

M. BRABANTIO   'I was Madam Brabantio in life.'

SOUN   'What brings you to this dark place?'

M. BRABANTIO   'I feel comfortable here. It suits me since I lost my daughter. And you? What brings you here?'

SOUN   'The same. I lost my son.'

M. BRABANTIO   'Who was he?'

SOUN   'A brave Commander named Othello.'

M. BRABANTIO   'Oh, no. Not he who murdered my daughter?'

SOUN   'Desdemona?'

M. BRABANTIO   'Yes.'

SOUN   'Are we enemies then?'

M. BRABANTIO   'Of course. Our vengeance is more molten than our sorrow.'

SOUN   'Yet, we have much to share. Clever, violent
                Othello.'

M. BRABANTIO   'Headstrong, passionate Desdemona.'

SOUN   'Both died in and for love.'

M. BRABANTIO   'Miserable. I prayed to Mother Mary for help
                when your son slaughtered my daughter.'

SOUN   'A waste. I spoke to my gods for guidance
                when, in remorse, my son responded with
                suicide.'

M. BRABANTIO   'Here are their graves. Let us kneel.'

SOUN   'Not yet. I come from a land wildly different
                from yours. A desert land pierced by forests
                of palm. There we obey nature and look to it
                for the language of the gods. We keep close
                the traditions they have taught us. One is our
                way of cleansing, of diluting the poisons life
                forces us to swallow.'

M. BRABANTIO   'And what is that way?'

SOUN   'An altar. We build an altar to the spirits who
                are waiting to console us.'

DONGORI
'Beautiful'
will be my plan.
Strong,
up to the task
and filled with pain.
Radiant,
I push back the hurt.
I harness myself
to every good thing
I can produce
whatever
my destiny.

Dongori,
violence.
Dongori,
obliteration.
Dongori,
enslavement.

Dongori,
I break the cord,
I undo the knot.

I free myself
from this vine of thorns.
At the heart of marriage
I grant myself
dignity
as my first
duty.

Today
I aspire to self-respect.
Mama,
do you understand me?
Today,
I aspire to self-esteem.
Papa,
will you forgive me?

6.

Who could have thought a military
commander, trained to let blood, would
be more, could be more, than a brutal arm
educated solely to kill?

I knew. How did I know?

We sat on a stone bench under an arch. I
remember the well of softness in his eyes.

And this is what he told:

OTHELLO   'As an orphan child a root woman adopted
me as her son and sheltered me from slavers.
I trailed her in forests and over sere as she
searched for medicinal plants, roots, and
flowers. She taught me some of her science.
How to breathe when there is no air.

Where water hid in cactus and certain vines.
She worshipped the natural world and
encouraged me to rehearse certain songs to
divine its power.

Yet soon I was captured by Syrians. I lived
with the camels and oxen and was treated
the same. I ate what I could find. It was
a happy day for me to be sold into an
army where food was regular and clothes
respectable. There I learned quickly the art
of arms and the strength of command. In
my first battle, I pointed my childish anger
with a daring completely strange to me. I
was happy, breathless and hungry for more
violent encounters. Only as a soldier could
I excel and turn the loneliness inside into
exhilaration.'

And this is what he told:

OTHELLO   'Our ship, upon an onslaught from land,
          sank. I alone was able to swim ashore. As
          I crawled along the beach I saw no enemy
          waiting on a ridge above the white sand. But
          I had heard the people of this place were
          invisible. Others said they were not invisible
          – they were chameleons able to assume
          the shades they inhabited. They could be
          detected only by their smell which meant
          in order to encounter their odor, one had
          to get close enough to be killed. I chose not
          to discover which was true: invisibility or
          camouflage. I knew there were tunnels in the
          sea. If you walk the beach and listen carefully
          you can hear the wind's music soughing
          from a certain kind of rock or swirl of sand.
          They signal an opening. Enter and a corridor
          of light shines in front of you, a hallway as
          dry as the Sahara, cool as the Himalayas. I
          waited in the light of that sea tunnel three
          days until the enemy believed me dead.'

And this is what he told:

OTHELLO   'There is an island surrounded by a lavender
ocean where fish leap into your boat, or you
can reach into the waves and catch them in
your hand; where trees bear fruit year round;
where birds speak as humans; where the
islanders have no heads and their faces are
settled in their chests. Once, desperate for
food and water, I was cast upon their shores.
Although they laughed at my deformity, at
the hilarity of my own head rising awkwardly
and vulnerably above my shoulders, they
were generous. They fed me and tended to
my needs. All human attributes were theirs
except for one: they could not sing for they
had no throats. When I sang for them the
songs the root woman had taught me, they
crowded about. Tears rolled down to their
waists as they wept their pleasure. It was
difficult to sail away, so awed was I by their
civilization.'

And this is what he told:

OTHELLO   'There are armies of women who kill men
                   in battles so fierce the moon itself hides from
                   the ribbons of shed blood. They cut off their
                   right breasts to ease the arrow shots of their
                   long bows to lethal precision. For this they
                   are called No-Breast or A-Mazon and must
                   remain virgins until after the first time they
                   kill a man. With male blood they stain their
                   hair and with his bone they sharpen their
                   arrowheads. Whole regiments fall before
                   them. They rule wooded nations and desert
                   kingdoms. Waters and precious stones have
                   their names. I have seen them and marveled
                   at their war skills.'

KEMEH BOURAMA
From your bloody battles
Dame Amazon,
could you bring me
the enemy's blood
so I can wash my face with it,
his intestines
so I can make a belt,
his skull
so I can make it
my throne?

The battle reaches its height.
Master of war
let your will be done.
Let his last victory be celebrated.
His victory over weakness,
cowardice, and mediocrity.
Let his courage be celebrated
here for the last time in his presence
and forever,
once he has been defeated
by what he has done.
The battle reaches its height.
Master of war
let your will be done.

And this is what he confessed:

OTHELLO   'Part, perhaps, most of the joy, the pleasure,
                 of battle I took as a child soldier came from
                 having comrades who were like me and who
                 loved the fresh green leaves we were given
                 to eat. Chewing them infused us with more
                 than courage: we were potent and indifferent
                 to blood, cries of pain, debasement – to life,
                 even our own. Rape was perfunctory. Death
                 our brother. It took capture, imprisonment
                 for months to be rid of the craving for the
                 leaves and to absorb what we had become.
                 The self loathing, however, could only be
                 quieted by the glint of honor an honorable
                 army provided. My acceptance into the
                 mighty forces of Venice was my salvation.
                 Since then, military justice coupled with
                 the virtue of the corps have guided me.
                 Your gaze, spilling pity and understanding,
                 embolden me giving me hope that this, my
                 secret, will be our bond.'

                 Those are the tales he told. Tales that
                 stopped my heart as much as they fired
                 my mind. Tales of horror and strange. I
                 was captured by love and the prospect of
                 inhabiting a broad original world where I
                 could compete with the Amazons.

7.

My husband knew Iago was lying,
manipulating, sabotaging. So why did he
act on obvious deceit? Brotherhood. The
quiet approval beamed from one male
eye to another. Bright, tight, camaraderie.
Like-mindedness born of the exchange of
musk; the buck's regard of the doe; the mild
contempt following her capture. The wide,
wild celebrity men find with each other
cannot compete with the narrow comfort of
a wife. Romance is always overshadowed
by brawn. The language of love is trivial
compared to the hidden language of men
that lies underneath the secret language they
speak in public. But real love, the love of an
Amazon, is not based on pretty language or
the secret sharing between males.

Remember your last confession? The last tale
you told?

OTHELLO   Aroused by bloodletting, Iago and I entered
a stable searching for food or drink. What
we found were two women cowering. After
a first glance, they never looked at us again.
They lowered their eyes and whimpered.
They were old, so old. Fingers gnarled by
years of brutal work; teeth random and softly
withering flesh. No matter. We took turns
slaking the thirst of our loins rather than
our throats. I don't know how long it lasted.
Our groans and their soft crying drape my
memory of passing time. Once sated, we
heard a noise behind us coming from a

heap of hay. We turned to see a child, a boy, staring wild-eyed at a scene that must have seemed to him a grotesque dream. Except for the women's whimpering, silence fell.

DESDEMONA   Surely, surely you did not assault the boy. Tell me you did not.

OTHELLO   No. We never touched nor threatened him.

DESDEMONA   Then mercy triumphed, at last.

OTHELLO   Not mercy at all.

DESDEMONA   What then?

OTHELLO   There was a look between us. Before our decision to do no more harm our eyes met, Iago's and mine, in an exchange of secrecy.

DESDEMONA   And of shame?

OTHELLO   Shame, yes.

DESDEMONA   The unspeakable is no longer. Now you have pried loose the screws twisting your tongue. The telling is itself courage.

OTHELLO   You don't understand. Shame, yes, but worse. There was pleasure too. The look between us was not to acknowledge shame, but mutual pleasure. Pleasure in the degradation we had caused; more pleasure in leaving a witness to it. We were not only refusing to kill our own memory, but insisting on its life in another.

DESDEMONA   That is obscene, monstrous.

OTHELLO   Without question. Yet there is another
               question, a vital one. Can you forgive me?

DESDEMONA   No, I cannot. But I can love you and remain
               committed to you.

OTHELLO   In spite of what I have described?

DESDEMONA   In addition to what you have described. Did
               you think loving another was a profit-driven
               harvest: choosing the ripe and discarding
               the rot? Love is complete, whole, fearless;
               otherwise it is merely a banquet, a feast
               planned to sate a hunger for variety, not
               commitment to one choice. Honest love does
               not cringe at the first roll of thunder; nor
               does it flinch when faced with the lightning
               flash of human sin. I always knew you
               were caressing me with fingers hardened
               by swords and that your hands stroking my
               breasts also drew blood. My error was in
               believing that you were more than the visage
               of your mind.

OTHELLO   I pray I am more.

DIANFA

Do you know what torments me?
Do you want to know my anguish?
I fear the ultimate betrayal.
Will you abandon me?
Honey and sweetness
will never be separated.
Its acrid taste
remains faithful to the dah.
The kaicedrat will never lose
its bitterness.

Don't leave me.
My power is so frail
here below.
In one way or another
my time
is coming to
an end.

For me, old age
would be a pleasure.
I would destroy
whatever death might spare.
You are nothing more
than a game.
A game in which
I would still like
to take part.

Grant me the time I need
for wisdom
to grow in me
and give me the strength
to smile at my pain.
Don't leave me.
Honey and sweetness
will never be separated.
Its acrid taste
remains faithful to the dah.
The kaicedrat will never lose
its bitterness.

Stay with me
for the time it takes
for me to conquer my fears,
to overcome my agony
You took back the substance
and the meaning you gave my life,
that rewarded my life.
Now, you abandon me
to nothingness.

8.

EMILIA   Well, well. If it isn't the martyr of Venice.
                 Remember me? We died together.
                 How do you do?

DESDEMONA   Emilia! I've wondered if I'd see you again.

EMILIA   Did you know I was the first to lay dying next
                 to you?

DESDEMONA   All is known here, though not always
                 understood.

EMILIA   What's left to understand? Both of us murdered,
                 we failed. Noble as we tried to be, we failed.

DESDEMONA   Failed? As women? Emilia, you confound me.
                 Didn't you acquiesce to all of Iago's demands,
                 even the most vile, corrupt ones? Yet you
                 admitted to me your willingness, eagerness
                 even, to betray your own husband if it led to
                 higher status. Your deception, your dangerous,
                 murderous silence led to my death. And it led
                 to yours.

EMILIA   Life is what it is. Women try to survive, since
                 we cannot flourish.

DESDEMONA   I wonder if collapse of virtue is not survival at
                 all but cowardice.

EMILIA   I resent that coming from one who had
                 no defense against lies or her husband's
                 strangling fingers.

DESDEMONA   And you, Emilia? You and I were friends,
but didn't the man you knelt to protect run
a gleaming sword through your survival
strategies?

EMILIA   And why did he? Because I befriended and
supported you. I exposed his lies, you ingrate!
That is your appreciation for my devotion to
you? 'My cloak, Emilia', 'My night gown,
Emilia.'

'Unpin me, Emilia.' 'Arrange my bed sheets,
Emilia.' That is not how you treat a friend;
that's how you treat a servant. Someone
beneath you, beneath your class which takes
devotion for granted.

DESDEMONA   It's true. I relied on your help and mistook it
for benevolence. I was deceived.

EMILIA   You always thought me deceptive, simply
because I would let myself be seduced in
order to gain higher status. To own my life I
had to forge a secret path.

DESDEMONA   Doesn't deception lead to ruin?

EMILIA   So does honesty, as your example shows. Like
you I believed marriage was my salvation.
It was not. Lust charged everything; satisfied
itself everywhere; signaled by handkerchiefs;
hid behind curtains. And all of that passion
generated nothing. Not an infant among us.
No progeny; no future. I was an orphan.
I learned what I had to and polished those
lessons daily. Otherwise the sorrow of
motherlessness coupled with childlessness
would have broken me.

DESDEMONA   Emilia, I wish I had known you when we
were children. You had no family. I had too
much. You had no mother. I had no mother's
love.

EMILIA   It's not the same. An orphan knows how
quickly love can be withdrawn; knows that
complete safety is a child's hopeless dream.

DESDEMONA   You are right to correct me. Instead of
judging, I should have been understanding.

EMILIA   Thank you for saying so. I am glad you
never knew how desperate life is for the
truly orphaned, our fear of losing our place.
The long hours of servility in the grand
halls of mistresses, the rush to hide from
lascivious men – including your husband –
the vulnerability, the ever-present danger. I
stared at the moon for guidance, at the sea
for answers.

They had none. Then, one day I saw a tiny
lizard dozing in sunlight. Suddenly her scales
seemed to move, to tremble. I watched as
she shed her dull outer skin; struggled, then
finally, crawled out of it, exposing that which
had been underneath – her jeweled self. No
one helped her; she did it by herself. What
struck me, more than the brilliance of her
new skin, was that she did not leave the outer
one behind. She dragged it with her. As
though the camouflage would still be needed
to disguise her true dazzle. That little lizard
changed my life.

9.

DESDEMONA	Barbary! Barbary. Come closer. How I have missed you. Remember the days we spent by the canal? We ate sweets and you saved the honey for me eating none yourself. We shared so much.
BARBARY	We shared nothing.
DESDEMONA	What do you mean?
SA'RAN	I mean you don't even know my name. Barbary? Barbary is what you call Africa. Barbary is the geography of the foreigner, the savage. Barbary? Barbary equals the sly, vicious enemy who must be put down at any price; held down at any cost for the conquerors' pleasure. Barbary is the name of those without whom you could neither live nor prosper.
DESDEMONA	So tell me. What is your name?
SA'RAN	Sa'ran.
DESDEMONA	Well, Sa'ran, whatever your name, you were my best friend.
SA'RAN	I was your slave.
DESDEMONA	What does that matter? I have known and loved you all my life.
SA'RAN	I am black-skinned. You are white-skinned.

DESDEMONA   So?

SA'RAN   So you don't know me. Have never known me.

DESDEMONA   Because of your skin? It is you who lack knowing. Think. I wed a Moor. I fled my home to be with him. I defied my father, all my family to wed him. I joined him on the battlefield.

SA'RAN   And he slaughtered you. Now do you know our difference?

DESDEMONA   And your lover slaughtered you as surely as if he had strangled you. Remember the song you sang every day until you wasted away and embraced death without fight or protest?

SA'RAN

The poor soul sat sighing by a sycamore tree,
Sing all a green willow;
Her hand on her bosom, her head on her knee.
Sing willow, willow, willow.
The fresh streams ran by her, and murmur'd her moans;
Sing willow, willow, willow;
Her salt tears fell from her and soften'd the stones;
Sing willow, willow, willow –

SA'RAN   Stop. Don't.

DESDEMONA   Listen to me.

SA'RAN   No, you listen. I have no rank in your world.
                I do what I am told. I brought you what you
                wanted before you knew you wanted it. I
                kissed your every cut and bruise. I held you
                when fever made you tremble, and when
                your parents made you weep. You never had
                to wash your hands or feet or face. I did that
                for you.

DESDEMONA   You blame?

SA'RAN   I clarify!

DESDEMONA   Sa'ran. We are women. I had no more
                control over my life than you had. My prison
                was unlike yours but it was prison still.

                Was I ever cruel to you? Ever?

SA'RAN   No. You never hurt or abused me.

DESDEMONA   Who did?

SA'RAN   You know who did. But I have thought
                long and hard about my sorrow. No more
                'willow'. Afterlife is time and with time there
                is change. My song is new:

'Someone leans near
And sees the salt my eyes have shed.
I wait, longing to hear
Words of reason, love or play
To lash or lull me toward the hollow day.
Silence kneads my fear
Of crumbled star-ash sifting down
Clouding the rooms here, here.
I shore up my heart to run. To stay.
But no sign or design marks the narrow way.
Then on my skin a sudden breath caresses
The salt my eyes have shed.
And I hear a call – clear, so clear:
"You will never die again."
What bliss to know
I will never die again.'

DESDEMONA   We will never die again.

10.

DESDEMONA   Your cloak is tattered.

OTHELLO   So am I.

DESDEMONA   Why, may I ask?

OTHELLO   The endlessness of time and the depth of regret equals hell.

OTHELLO   I always wanted to know why you stopped struggling when I encircled your throat and cut off your breath. Why did you let my rage run free? Why did you deny I murdered you?

DESDEMONA   You were not killing me. You were killing Othello. The man I believed you to be was lost to me. So what was left to struggle for?

OTHELLO   Tell me about this Othello you believed me to be.

DESDEMONA   More than the rapture of his body; more than the sword at his side. My Othello is not the man who chose to believe what you must have known was false.

OTHELLO   It's clear now. You never loved me. You fancied the idea of me, the exotic foreigner who kills for the State, who will die for the State. Everyone I slaughtered was someone who wanted your head on a pike. How comforting it must have been – protected

by a loyal black warrior. What excited
you was my strange story: enslaved youth
ruined by war then redeemed by it, fantastic
adventures, stories of freaks and miracles.
A confession known only to you, my wife.
And you thought that was all there was to
me – a useful myth, a fairy's tale cut to suit
a princess' hunger for real life, not the dull
existence of her home.

DESDEMONA   You are wrong! You believed a lie. You broke
my hymen and thought I was unfaithful the
next day? Me?

OTHELLO   I don't know. I did suspect. Actually I don't
care. Listen to me. More than infidelity
my rage was toward your delusion. Your
requirements for a bleached, ultra-civilized
soul framed in blood, for court manners
honed by violence. Have you any idea
what it took to get to the position I held?
Who sabotaged me, delayed promotions,
took credit for my victories? Who fed
rumors about my intelligence, my virility,
my character? Even with the gore of their
enemies, the smell of it, the drips of it on my
sword, their contempt over-powered what
should have been glistening gratitude. Only
perseverance, discipline and a shrewd sense
of what truly matters kept me going. While
you played with my reality; toyed with it;
turned it into – into spectacle.

CASSIO interrupts.

CASSIO   Speaking of spectacle, I reckon it is superior
to a feeble reality, especially one that has
collapsed and become a barely controlled
nightmare. Those in charge of defending the

State slew one another like rival scorpions,
abusing their former comrades with deceit
and fury. But first came the poison of weak,
disloyal women. Fair Desdemona? Innocent
Desdemona? Hah! I have touched her
and she neither screamed nor slapped my
hands away. Then, to hurry the demise,
came that vain, arrogant Othello, swanning
about above his station and way above his
geography and his history. A dangerous
godless mix, unable to govern, to know
with certainty what is best for the State. I
am compelled now to repeal and replace
whatever they have initiated into law.

Dissolute. It's true. That is the word that
accurately describes my youth. Four liters of
wine I consumed before the sun touched the
top of heaven. Following its descent, well, I
couldn't tell anyone how much I drank. The
point is, it not only didn't interfere with my
duties, it helped me execute them. But when
I gave up brew, I was promoted by Othello;
then demoted by him. Why? I was tricked
into drunkenness! I relied too heavily on
my intimacy with Desdemona, hoping she
would make Othello give me back my job.
Then tricked again with the theft of a dirty
handkerchief. Finally wounded by the man I
believed my friend.

I acknowledge Othello was competent, even
intelligent. I understand he had vision. But of
what value is either in day-to-day rule? Who
needs vision to declare war and win it at all
costs? The needs of the State are mundane,
and therein safety lies.

The arrogance of that Moor riles me still.
Undermining him improves my status daily
and solidifies my power.

Now Cyprus is under my reign. I am the one
who decides. Othello gone from life; Iago
suffering in a prison cell. A clean sweep that
allows me to rule and perhaps help Venice
return to its prominence. Wars will be won,
not abandoned. Perhaps a stumble here and
there; some resisting voices of course, but
their subtlety will merely produce confusion.

So let me be clear. Power is more than
responsibility; it is destiny. Destiny few men
are able to handle. While there may be so-
called 'slaughter of the innocents' in its wake,
none of that will deter me. I bow, modestly,
to destiny's demands. Me alone. I am its
servant and it is mine.

DESDEMONA   To think I tried to save him. I was wrong, so
wrong. Was Cassio always such a fool?

OTHELLO   Always. He enrages me as much now as he
did then. But I hid my fury and overlooked
his fatal ignorance because I believed him
loyal. Fidelity is a necessity in the military.
Lives depend on it, but I could not. I was
doubted and deceived at every turn. Why?
Because I am African? Because I was sold
into slavery? Or because I was better than
they? Whatever the reason, I had to prove
myself over and over again. Cassio's fawning
I welcomed in that malign atmosphere, until
lies from every quarter infected me and
disturbed the balance of my mind.

DESDEMONA   I apologize for a profound error in judgment.

OTHELLO   Apology is a pale word for what I am called upon to recognize. I am beyond sorry; it is shame that strafes me. And shame too for diminishing our life together as spectacle. It was never that.

DESDEMONA   True. Yet Cassio lives to rule and we do not because love cannot survive without trust.

Your doubt and my righteousness mangled our love.

OTHELLO   We should have had such honest talk, not fantasy, the evening we wed.

My love for you was mind deep.

I murdered myself and you to stop the drama. If I could slay myself again, I would. But afterlife forbids a double death.

DESDEMONA   I am sick of killing as a solution. It solves nothing. Questions nothing, produces nothing, nothing, but more of itself. You thought war was alive, had honor and reason. I tell you it is well beyond all that. My mistake was believing that you hated war as much as I did. You believed I loved Othello the warrior. I did not.

I was the empire you had already conquered.

Alone together we could have been invincible.

OTHELLO   And now? Together? Alone? Is it too late?

DESDEMONA   'Late' has no meaning here. Here there is
only the possibility of wisdom.

Of knowing the earth is not quiet nor
waiting. In the screech of color and the
whisper of the lightless depths of the sea,
it boils, breaks or slumbers. And in this
restless rest human life is as unlimited and
miraculous as love. Here the infidel can
embrace the saint just as sunlight creates the
air we breathe.

KÉLÉ MANDI
When two beings meet,
each brings to the other a bit of themselves.
So we learn, we construct our selves, we evolve.
I bring what makes me different from you.
Give me a bit of what you are.
But do it with gentleness and tolerance,
since all that you impose upon me with force
will only leave the imprint
of your violence and your arrogance.
One can't force the other
to accept what is offered.
In accepting what you have to give,
I open you to what I have to offer.

DESDEMONA   The world is alive and even if we kill it, it
returns fresh, full-throated and hungry for
time and space in which to thrive. And if
we haven't secured the passionate peace we
yearn for, it is because we haven't imagined
it. Is it still available, this human peace? In
our privileged position in timelessness, our
answer is a roar.

If it's a question
of working together
on the task,
I would be happy to take part.
Whether we are from the same place or not.
Whether we are from the same culture or not.
Should we celebrate this moment?
It would fill me with joy.

Must we discuss,
understand each other,
and decide?
I would be yours.
It would fill me with joy.
But for now,
while we talk,
I know that I can only shine
in the light of adversity
that opposes
my self
and my vices.

DESDEMONA   We will be judged by how well we love.

My pride,
my foolish pride in being human
disgusts me.
It is the source of so much evil.
I have no ambition to exist
in this world
except as an impermanent
element
facing eternity
with no choice
but to burn
then finish
one way
or another.

Toni Morrison

Toni Morrison was awarded the Nobel Prize for Literature in 1993. She is the author of many novels, including *The Bluest Eye*, *Beloved* (made into a major film), *Paradise* and, most recently, *Home*. She has also received the National Book Critics Circle Award and a Pulitzer Prize for her fiction. In addition to *Desdemona* her theatrical work includes writing the text for *Margaret Garner* (music composed by Richard Danielpour), and *Dreaming Emmett* an unpublished play directed by Gilbert Moses and performed at the Marketplace Capitol Repertory Theater of Albany. Ms. Morrison has written lyrics for Kathleen Battle (commissioned by Carnegie Hall), Sylvia McNair, Jessye Norman and André Previn. Ms. Morrison founded the Princeton Atelier which for fifteen years has brought actors, composers, writers and artists of all genres together to work with students on the artists' own projects. Several of her novels including *The Bluest Eye* have been adapted for the stage.

Rokia Traoré

Delicate, intense and gifted with extraordinary presence, Rokia Traoré has created her own unmistakable style and sound, crafting a musical universe with deep roots in traditional Mali transformed by inspired, spontaneous elements of the avant-garde, rhythm and blues, and rock and roll. Daring and fresh, she moves, sings and writes with a natural authority centered in serenity and strength. Her voice is timeless, inviting audiences into a profoundly personal emotional world, a dream, a trance, with surprising and delicious bursts of dance party energy. That illuminated mix of high spirits and meditative focus empower her to speak with courage and with grace about difficult topics, and power the momentum and determination that carries her music forward through deeply felt sadness into a realm that is visionary and healing.

First winning the Radio France International (RFI) *Discoveries Award* for Africa in 1997, the next year she was the revelation of the Festival Musiques Métisses d'Angoulême. By the time Rokia Traoré was twenty-five, many leading African musicians, including the legendary Ali Farka Touré, recognized her as one of the great African voices of the future. Her first albums, *Mouneïssa*, *Wanita* and *Bowmboï* (with guests ranging from Toumani Diabaté to the Kronos Quartet) are now classics. Her latest album, *Tchamantché*, took the French *Victoires de la musique* award for the best World Music album of the year 2009.

Her originality, innovation and eclecticism have moved her beyond 'world music' categories – she has always been adventurous in her choice of collaborators, creating refined and subtle cross-cultural projects with deep integrity, fineness of detail and startling emotional precision. It was while working on a special commission for the 250th birthday of Mozart in Vienna's New Crowned Hope Festival curated by Peter Sellars in 2006, that she first met Toni Morrison. *Desdemona* reunites her with these colleagues several years later. In addition to her international touring and recording work, at home in Mali, she has founded the Passerelle Foundation devoted to supporting the next generation of Malian musicians.

Peter Sellars

Opera, theatre and festival director Peter Sellars is one of the most innovative and powerful forces in the performing arts in America and abroad. A visionary artist, Sellars is known for ground-breaking interpretations of classic works. Whether it is Mozart, Handel, Shakespeare, Sophocles, or the sixteenth-century Chinese playwright Tang Xianzu, Peter Sellars strikes a universal chord with audiences, engaging and illuminating contemporary social and political issues.

Sellars has staged operas at the Glyndebourne Festival, the Lyric Opera of Chicago, the Netherlands Opera, the Opéra National de Paris, the Salzburg Festival, the San Francisco Opera and Teatro Real (Madrid), among others, establishing a reputation for bringing twentieth-century and contemporary operas to the stage, including works by Olivier Messiaen, Paul Hindemith and György Ligeti. Inspired by the compositions of Kaija Saariaho, Osvaldo Golijov and Tan Dun, he has guided the creation of productions of their work that have expanded the repertoire of modern opera. Sellars has been a driving force in the creation of many new works with longtime collaborator composer John Adams, including *Nixon in China*, *The Death of Klinghoffer*, *El Niño*, *Doctor Atomic* and *A Flowering Tree*. A staging of their latest work, *The Gospel According to the Other Mary*, will be seen in the US and Europe early in 2013.

A Harvard graduate, Sellars was appointed Artistic Director of the American National Theater at the John F. Kennedy Center for the Performing Arts in Washington, DC, at the age of twenty-six, where between 1984 and 1986 he originated seven productions and presented eighteen others from a wide range of American and international theatre companies. His landmark ANT staging of Sophocles' *Ajax*, set at the Pentagon, was invited to tour Europe and ignited the start of an international career. Other noteworthy theatre projects include a 1994 staging of Shakespeare's *The Merchant of Venice* set in southern California with a cast of Black, white, Latino and Asian-American actors; an Antonin Artaud radio play coupled with the poetry of June Jordan, *For an End to the Judgment of God/Kissing God Goodbye*, staged as a press conference on the war in Afghanistan; a production of Euripides' *The Children of Herakles*, focusing on contemporary immigration and refugee issues and experience; and, in 2009, *Othello*, inspired by and set in the America of newly elected President Barack Obama.

Desdemona, Sellars' collaboration with the Nobel Prize-winning novelist Toni Morrison and Malian composer and singer Rokia Traoré, was performed in Vienna, Brussels, Paris, Berkeley, New York and Berlin in 2011, and presented in London as part of the 2012 Cultural Olympiad.

Sellars has led several major arts festivals, including the 1990 and 1993 Los Angeles Festivals; the 2002 Adelaide Arts Festival in Australia; and the 2003 Venice Biennale International Festival of Theatre in Italy. In 2006 he was Artistic Director of New Crowned Hope, a month-long festival in Vienna for which he invited international artists from diverse cultural backgrounds to create new work in the fields of music, theater, dance, film, the visual arts and architecture for the city of Vienna's Mozart Year celebrating the 250th anniversary of Mozart's birth.

Sellars is a professor in the Department of World Arts and Cultures at UCLA and Resident Curator of the Telluride Film Festival. He is the recipient of a MacArthur Fellowship, the Erasmus Prize, the Sundance Institute Risk-Takers Award and the Gish Prize, and is a member of the American Academy of Arts and Sciences.